JESUS:
History's Incomparable Man?

Was He?

WILLIAM C. SAVAGE

ACW Press
Phoenix, Arizona 85013

Jesus:
History's Incomparable Man?
Copyright ©2001 William C. Savage
All rights reserved

Cover Design by Alpha Advertising
Interior design by Pine Hill Graphics

Published by ACW Press
5501 N. 7th Ave., #502
Phoenix, Arizona 85013
www.acwpress.com
The views expressed or implied in this work may not necessarily reflect those of ACW Press. Ultimate design, content, and editorial accuracy of this work is the responsibility of the author.

Publisher's Cataloging-in-Publication
(Provided by Quality Books, Inc.)

Savage, William C.
    Jesus : history's incomparable man? / by William C. Savage. -- 1st ed.
    p. cm.
    ISBN 1-892525-49-6

    1. Jesus Christ--Person and offices. 2. Jesus Christ --Biography. I. Title

BT303.S28 2001   232.9
                              QBI01-200328

All rights reserved. No part of this book may be reproduced, stored in a retrieval system, or transmitted in any form or by any means—electronic, mechanical, photocopying, recording, or otherwise—without prior permission in writing from the copyright holder except as provided by USA copyright law.

Printed in the United States of America.

Dedicated

To those with inquiring minds

Table of Contents

A Note from the Author 7

1. *Long Prophesied* 9
2. *Born of Virgin* 17
3. *Son of God* 21
4. *An Appointed Name* 23
5. *Supernatural Events Accompanying Birth*. 25
6. *Miracle Worker*. 29
7. *All-Knowing* 33
8. *Sinless*. 37
9. *Foretold Future*. 41
10. *Offer of Forgiveness*. 47
11. *Salvation by Grace* 51
12. *Supernatural Events Surrounding Death* 55
13. *The Resurrection*. 61
14. *Kingdom of Love*. 67
15. *Second Coming*. 71
    Conclusion. 75

A Note from the Author

The person Jesus of Nazareth has been the subject of more literature, more art, more music and more study than anybody who has ever lived. History itself is divided by this life, time being measured as being before (B.C.) or after (A.D.) his days on earth. Yet for many, their knowledge about this man who lived in Palestine from approximately 3 B.C. to A.D. 30 is often sketchy, mistaken or nonexistent.

One may ask, "Is it possible that history has produced one incomparable life?" "Is there a simple, accurate way of knowing what it is about this man that sets him apart?" For those with such questions, this little book seeks to assemble, in a concise, easy-to-read format, the objective data that collectively suggests Jesus' uniqueness—thus offering a means by which the reader may draw an informed conclusion of his or her own about whether this man deserves to be held in pre-eminence.

CHAPTER ONE

Long Prophesied

*P*erhaps the most dramatic way in which Jesus might be different from all humankind is that upwards of forty specific, historical details of his birth, life and death were foretold in writing hundreds of years prior to the fact.

From approximately 2,000 B.C., ancient writers across some fifteen hundred years set out multiple prophecies about a person who was to be specially appointed by God to be the redeemer of mankind, the Messiah. These writings have been available throughout the centuries, having been included in a collection of Hebrew scriptures known as the Old Testament of the Holy Bible. When later Jesus lived on the earth, it was found that he had become the first person to fulfil historically each of those prophecies—essentially a mathematical impossibility.

Examples of the advance details in the Old Testament about "the Holy One"—his birth, life, death—are set out below:

In Birth.

Though he was to be a Nazarene (from Nazareth), he would be born in Bethlehem of Judea.

His family line, set forth in advance, was to include Noah, Shem, Abram, Isaac, Jacob, the tribe of Judah, the Hebrew nation, Jesse, and King David—all well-known figures in history.

In the first century A.D., a tax collector, Matthew, traced and recorded Jesus' genealogy forward across forty-three generations, from

Abraham through King David to Jesus' birth. Matthew stated his purpose was to show that Jesus was born heir to the throne of David, as Isaiah had said the Messiah would be. This record may be found at the outset of the New Testament of the Holy Bible.

In the first century, a medical doctor, Luke, traced Jesus' genealogy backward through seventy-six generations to Adam, the first known human being. This lineage includes all the names mentioned above and is also found in the New Testament.

Of note, the Messianic bloodline stopped with Jesus. Since he had no children, and since meticulous Jewish genealogies back to antiquity are no longer kept, it is not possible for anybody born later to trace his family line back to the ninth century B.C. (King David) and beyond, through the above required lineage, to lay genetic claim to being the Messiah.

In Life.

The predicted one would preach good news to the meek, heal the brokenhearted, proclaim freedom for the captives (spiritual and physical), open the eyes of the blind, proclaim the year of the Lord's favor and the day of his vengeance, comfort all who mourn.

He would be a prophet like Moses.

He would benefit Gentiles (non-Israelites), as well as his own people, the Israelites.

He would be exalted and extolled.

He would at one and the same time be acknowledged as a king, yet would ride upon a lowly colt of a donkey.

He would have a variety of titles ascribed to him, such as Messiah, the Holy One, Jehovah, Judge, Lawgiver, the Prince of Peace, King, Witness, The Lord Our Righteousness, Mighty One, Redeemer, Son of Righteousness, Elect of God, the Lord God.

In Death.

His death and mission were foretold at length and in graphic detail. He was to be a saviour, a sin-bearer, a suffering redeemer.

He would be despised, rejected of men.

Kings and rulers would plot against him. False witnesses would rise up against him. He would be silent before his accusers.

A friend would betray him.

He would be sold for thirty pieces of silver.

The money would be used to buy a parcel of land from a potter.

He would be a man of sorrows, oppressed, spat upon, afflicted, stricken of God.

He would be pierced in his hands and feet (a graphic prophecy of death by crucifixion, made hundreds of years before the Romans practiced crucifixion).

His back would be beaten; his body would be mutilated.

In his agony, oppressors would offer him gall for meat, vinegar for drink.

Out of love, he would pray for his enemies.

He would die among the wicked, be buried with the rich.

His garments would be divided among oppressors; but for his robe, they (soldiers) would cast lots.

People would be astonished at his marred, contorted body.

This catalog of prophetic details prompts two questions:

> Does the world's historical literature reveal such highly specific and unusual details being prophesied about the birth, life and death of anybody else?

> Does history tell us of any other life that has fulfilled all these prophecies, written hundreds of years before the fact?

One suggested explanation for this phenomenon of foretelling and fulfilment is that these specific details might have been given in advance so that humankind may correctly identify the arrival of God's specially appointed redeemer, the Messiah.

Did this man admit to being the Messiah? Just before being crucified, when the ruling high priest insisted Jesus declare whether he was the Christ (Messiah), he confessed, "I am."

CHAPTER TWO

Born of Virgin

*I*n the mid-eighth century B.C., a statesman-prophet, Isaiah, wrote, "The Lord Himself shall give you a sign, 'Behold a virgin shall conceive, and bear a son.'" Across the centuries, this pronouncement has been considered a foretelling of the divinely promised Messiah. Since virginal conception was an impossibility apart from God's supernatural intervention, it was a "sign" that could be given humankind only by the Lord.

In 3–5 B.C., a baby was born in Palestine to a woman who claimed she had never had sexual relations with a man. Some eight months prior to the birth, she reported to her cousin Elizabeth (and to Elizabeth's husband, Zacharias) that she had been surprised by an angel coming to her, saying that she would conceive, give birth to a son, and should call his name "Jesus." Upon her inquiring of the angel, "How shall this be since I have known (sexually) no man?" the angel answered, "The power of the Highest shall come upon you, hence the child shall be called the Son of God."

The birth took place in Bethlehem of Judah. The mother was a woman of Nazareth in Galilee, named Mary. The baby was a son. She named him "Jesus," as the angel instructed.

When Mary's fiancé learned of her pregnancy, his first reaction was to avoid inevitable public disgrace by terminating the engagement. Ultimately, however, Joseph proceeded with marriage and later fathered children of his own by Mary. He reported that his change of mind was the result of an angel coming to him, telling him that Mary's conception was of the Holy Spirit, that he should marry her without fear, and that the pending birth would be the fulfilment of Isaiah's virgin-birth prophecy.

Is there any other evidence of Jesus' birth by a virgin? Perhaps circumstantial reasoning sheds light:

> It seems unlikely Mary and Joseph would have gone back to live in their hometown, Nazareth, had they been fornicators and had their son been a bastard.

> Not to accept the testimony of Mary and Joseph would be to discredit an otherwise exemplary couple.

> There is no account of Jesus being ridiculed as a bastard, illegitimate.

> Several other children, known by name, were born to Mary and Joseph. Jesus, Mary's firstborn, was the only child they said was virgin-born.

> It is unlikely Jesus would have had a popular following, had he been illegitimate.

> If a divine person were to come into the world through a human mother, might a supernatural conception/birth be expected?

Of note, one of the written accounts of this medical miracle was recorded by an eminent physician, Luke. He stated, "I, myself, have investigated everything carefully from the beginning, including reports from the first eyewitnesses, that you might know the exact truth (about Jesus)."

CHAPTER THREE

Son of God

If Jesus was born without a human father, is there any objective evidence that *God* was uniquely his father? Are we limited to the accounts given first by Mary and later by Joseph that an angel had privately told each that the child would be conceived by God's Holy Spirit, and thus be the "Son of God"?

On two occasions, people assembled outdoors heard "a voice from heaven" announcing Jesus' unique, divine sonship:

At the onset of Jesus' three-year ministry, he asked to be baptized by John the Baptizer. Finding John at the River Jordan baptizing people who had come from Jerusalem and all Judea and the regions around Jordan, Jesus too submitted to baptism. On coming out of the water, a voice from heaven exclaimed, "This is my beloved Son, in whom I am well pleased."

In the third year of his ministry, Jesus took three of his disciples to a mountaintop to pray. Peter, James and John later reported having had a frightening experience in which a voice out of the cloud said, "This is my beloved Son, hear him."

If by these two unprecedented heaven-to-earth pronouncements God was declaring Jesus to be uniquely his Son, does it follow that Jesus was uniquely divine, and does it follow that Jesus was uniquely a heaven-sent emissary invested with the authority of carrying out on earth the intentions of his heavenly Father?

CHAPTER FOUR

An Appointed Name

When Isaiah prophesied in the 700s B.C. that a son would be born of a virgin (see chapter 2), he included an additional statement that her son's name would be called "Emmanuel." In the Hebrew language, Emmanuel translates to "God with us."

In 3–5 B.C., when Joseph reported that an angel of the Lord appeared to him in a dream (see chapter 2), he added that he was instructed to call his fiancée Mary's soon-to-be-born son, "Jesus." This name means "God is salvation," or "He shall save His people from their sins."

Joseph claimed the angel said, "Jesus" fulfils "Emmanuel." The two names are said to explain interrelated roles for the same person. "Jesus" describes purpose, in particular, God saves. "Emmanuel" describes function, namely God with us. Hence: God "saves" by being "with us."

The right name was seemingly an essential credential for being the long-predicted, specially appointed one from God. Hence, a person with any other name would be disqualified from being God's Messiah.

CHAPTER FIVE

Supernatural Events Accompanying Birth

Jesus' coming into this world was attended by audible and visible announcements from heaven. These are dramatic happenings of a type unknown elsewhere in recorded history.

Several shepherds reported that while tending their sheep in the field one night, they were encountered by an angel of the Lord in bright light and by a multitude of heavenly host. The angel proclaimed that the Christ, the Lord, had been born that day in the city of Bethlehem. He then told the shepherds they could distinguish the baby by two peculiarities: The child would be lying in a cattle feed-trough instead of a crib and would be wrapped in cloths held together with bandages.

Did this angelic visitation really take place? Did these rugged ranchers believe this seemingly far-fetched story? On going to Bethlehem to verify for themselves, they found the baby just as was told them, and broadcast the astonishing episode widely.

In another region, wise men from the east reported seeing a unique star which they claimed signaled the birth of the King of the Jews. In their search for the Christ, they reported the star directed them and their servants across the treacherous desert to Jerusalem and ultimately to the same child in Bethlehem.

That this unprecedented story really took place is confirmed factually. King Herod insisted on meeting the wise men upon their entering Jerusalem, and then to protect his throne from challenge from a divinely appointed king, he ordered the assassination of all babies in Bethlehem two years old and younger. Worth pondering is the fact that this historical slaughter had been referred to six hundred years previously, by the prophet Jeremiah. Just prior to the massacre, an angel forewarned Jesus' parents of Herod's intention and instructed them to flee to Egypt for the remainder of Herod's life. Years later, when Jesus' parents obeyed another angel's instruction that it was now safe to return to their hometown of Nazareth, two more prophecies about the Christ recorded centuries previously were fulfilled: "He shall be called a Nazarene," and "Out of Egypt have I called My Son."

Do these acts of divine intervention surrounding Jesus' birth and childhood— witnessed by followers and non-followers alike—suggest again that Jesus has been set apart from all who have walked this earth?

CHAPTER SIX

Miracle Worker

Various witnesses have recorded that Jesus performed physical miracles—some thirty-seven in number.

What is a true miracle? The word "miracle" is frequently and mistakenly applied to a remarkable event which is unexpected and often inexplicable. At its root, a true miracle is an event in the physical world which deviates from the laws of nature. Hence, it is an event which must be wrought by supernatural agency, that is, by God himself.

From the accounts of Jesus' thirty-seven miracles, found in the historical writings of Matthew, Mark, Luke and John, one discovers the following:

All of Jesus' miracles were observed by multiple witnesses. Often they were performed in a crowd. On one occasion five thousand men, plus women and children, saw Jesus multiply five loaves and two fish into enough food to feed them all, with twelve basketfuls left over.

Jesus' miracles demonstrated instantaneous control of nature, marine life, weather, health and death: from walking on the sea, to turning water into wine; from stilling a life-threatening storm, to stilling a frantic demonic, sending the exorcised demons into a herd of some two thousand swine (which ran abruptly into a lake to their death); from producing tax money in a fish per his prophecy, to producing fish to overflowing in the nets of fishermen who had toiled all night and caught nothing; from restoring a soldier's severed ear, to restoring life to dead people on three different occasions (once raising the dead son of a widow from Nain before a crowd; once raising the twelve-year-old daughter of a ruler, Jairus, resulting in the witnessing throng spreading Jesus' fame abroad; once raising a man, Lazarus, who had been dead four days, bound with graveclothes and buried in a cave). These miracles, coupled with "many other" widely known miracles, resulted in Jerusalem's religious leaders conferring how they might put Jesus to death. Exclaiming, "The world is gone after him", they feared "all people would defect from their religion and believe on him."

Other of Jesus' miracles involved the full restoration of people with various afflictions: leprosy (ten men), blindness (two men), dumbness, dropsy, paralysis, crippled bodies, demon-possession, crippled hands and epilepsy. In all cases, Jesus performed his miracles instantaneously: he simply spoke a command and the healing or event in nature took place.

Why did Jesus perform these miracles? When asked if he was the long-awaited one from God, his answer was, "Tell the people what things you have seen and heard: how the blind see, the lame walk, the lepers are cleansed, the deaf hear, the dead are raised."

CHAPTER SEVEN

All-Knowing

*P*rofessors often say the most intelligent of humans know no more than 5 percent of all that is knowable. Some of the people who observed Jesus most closely proclaimed, "He knows all things."

It can be observed that:

On contemporary issues, he seemed to have full and perfect knowledge of whatever subject was at hand. He never displayed partial knowledge, never speculated, never was said to speak in error.

Of other realms, Jesus often spoke about knowing God intimately; about being with God before the world was; about the physical place of heaven, including many details; about knowing personally people who lived on earth in antiquity, such as Abraham, Moses, Elijah.

Several recorded incidents show that Jesus knew the unknowable, such as...

Describing details about peoples' lives the moment they first met;

Telling people their private thoughts before they spoke;

Describing peoples' whereabouts before being told;

Telling others the exact words they had spoken when they first heard of Jesus;

Knowing who, when and where opponents were secretly lying in wait;

Seeing a man under a fig tree in another part of town; and

Knowing he would be denied publicly by a follower he pre-identified.

Also, he knew what foreign object was inside a fish's stomach before it had been caught, and knew a certain animal was standing in a certain location in another town, before he arrived.

Of note, when Jesus uttered the type of things which would be impossible for an ordinary human to know, he didn't parade it as a stunt; nor did he posture as a psychic. Rather, he spoke these things in a matter-of-fact manner, as one might expect if he were in fact coexistent with God, as claimed.

CHAPTER EIGHT

Sinless

*F*rom all that is factual, Jesus appears to have been at all points godlike in thought, disposition and deed.

Pontius Pilate, the Roman governor of Judea, put Jesus on trial before his accusers, namely the religious leaders and their followers. After listening to the prosecution's charges, Pilate three times pronounced Jesus free of all wrong, saying, "I find no fault in this man," and "What evil has he done?"

Herod Antipas, chief ruler of Galilee, tried Jesus before an array of opponents and found him to be without fault.

Pilate's wife said, "He is a just man; do not condemn him."

One of the thieves crucified alongside Jesus exclaimed, "This man has done nothing wrong."

Various of the closest observers of Jesus' life, on different occasions said, "He knew no sin"; "was without sin, though tempted in all points as we are"; "was holy, harmless, undefiled, separate from sinners"; "without blemish, without spot"; "did no sin"; "in him is no sin."

Sin means "missing the mark" of God's standard of perfection. More broadly, sin is an inner disposition that seeks independence from God.

Jesus proclaimed his own sinlessness, saying, "I do always those things that please God," and "I have kept my Father's commandments and abide in His love." To an unsympathethic crowd, he challenged, "Which of you convicts me of sin?"

The Holy Bible quotes God as saying, "All have sinned," and "If any says he has not sinned, the truth is not in him." Since each member of the human race has exhibited the universal malady of sin in his or her own life, it follows that a person without sin would be generically different from all other humans.

In appproximately 700 B.C., a writing described as a prophecy about the coming Messiah identifies one of his distinguishing characteristics as, "He did no guile, neither was deception found on his lips." Hence, the actions and speech of this one were to be without sin.

CHAPTER NINE

Foretold Future

Given man's many remarkable capabilities, he does not however possess the capability to predict the future. When he guesses about future events, he occasionally guesses correctly; far more often, he is wrong—wrong even though his guesses are typically couched in generalities and lacking in detail.

Jesus frequently foretold the future. One notes that his utterances covered a wide range of topics, and included much detail. All his predictions intended for the following two centuries have come to pass, and in the manner he foretold.

Does such knowledge of the future distinguish Jesus from all others known to have lived on this planet? Does this superhuman capability define Jesus as being more than human?

In sacred writings of the eighth century B.C., God is quoted as saying that the ability to declare things before they come to pass is a power only God has. God in fact challenges any would-be gods to "produce your cause...and show things that are to come hereafter, that we may know whether the gods are divine."

Examples of Jesus' foretelling:

Of National Significance. Jesus foretold the total destruction of King Herod's splendorous temple and its adjacent buildings, that "not a stone would be left upon another," some thirty-seven years before Roman emperor Titus' seige actually caused that to happen.

On another occcasion, Jesus foretold that a friend would betray him—also that one of his closest disciples would deny him (three times), and that the third denial would be followed by the crowing of a cock (two times). At the time he uttered these prophecies, Jesus identified both parties by name, and in their presence. Each man strenuously rejected the possibility of his being a traitor, but in time acted just as Jesus had said he would.

Of International Significance. Jesus foretold that under military force the Jews would be suppressed, taken away from their native Israel and Judah and led into all nations, but that in the latter days, they would return. Both predictions have come to pass. Most notably the Jews were expelled by Titus in A.D. 70 and began returning in significant numbers after the United Nations decree of A.D. 1948 establishing the state of Israel.

Of His Message. Jesus foretold that his gospel would spread and be preached in all the world, and that followers throughout the world would be persecuted and killed. (Facts at beginning of twenty-first century: Approximately two billion of the earth's estimated six billion population profess to be followers of Jesus [world's largest religious following]; approximately 135,000 Christians are martyred annually for their faith.)

Of His Death. Perhaps most remarkable is the detail with which Jesus described the way in which he would die. On several occasions Jesus showed he knew in advance the assorted events that would accompany his death.

Location of his death—"Jerusalem"

Time of his death—Following his time of prayer on a specific day

Category of his death—"Slain", not natural causes

Cause of his death—"Betrayed by a friend"

Agents of his death—"Wicked men, religious authorities"

Reason for his death—"Rejected by three religious groups: Sanhedrin, Sadducees, Pharisees"

Preliminary to his death—"Multiple sufferings, scourging"

Type of death—"Crucifixion"

Company in death—"Associated with transgressors"

Aftermath of his death—"Arise from the dead, in three days"

Noteworthy is that these were events over which a victim would have no human control—events performed by people other than Jesus, events often caused by opponents who would have liked to prevent anything confirming of his divinity. All came to pass...just as Jesus foretold.

Remarkably, Jesus made no physical move to avoid any of these hideous death events. Rather, he said, "These things must happen, that the scriptures (of hundreds of years previous) might be fulfilled."

Bystanders often exclaimed, "Did ever a man speak like this?" Is there any satisfactory explanation beyond his own, that of being the Messiah, the Son of God?

CHAPTER TEN

Offer of Forgiveness

Unique among the world's religious leaders is the offer Jesus makes to forgive sin. Sin, that inner compulsion to disregard one's Maker, that urge to order one's life *by* oneself and *for* oneself, is that inner pull which inflicts every living person, causing one's estrangement from God. Humankind's core problem!

Commonly, world religions and philosophies are silent about sin, deny it, excuse it or try to explain it away. Jesus claimed to be capable and desirous of forgiving sin. He implied there is forgiveness in none other, because nobody else fulfills the two essential conditions for forgiving sin. First, the forgiver must be God Himself. Second, the forgiver must himself pay the penalty for the offense—which in the case of sin is death. Did Jesus demonstrate he possessed these dual qualifications?:

1. When Jesus offered to forgive sin, his opponents flaunted the well-known fact that only God has authority to forgive sin, because the root sin is an attitude and act against God. Jesus agreed! He proclaimed before a mixed multitude, "That you may know the Son of Man has power on earth to forgive sin," he would perform a feat they knew could be performed only by God. Before their eyes, Jesus commanded a man bedridden with paralysis, "Rise up and walk." They were amazed when immediately the man arose, took up his bed and walked off to his home.

2. God's ages-old law states, "The soul that sins, it shall die." When a person sins, the sinner pays the penalty and dies eternally, unless in mercy, God (the one sinned against) forgives and himself pays the penalty which justice before the law requires: death. Before a multitude, Jesus demonstrated just such an extraordinary forgiveness when he allowed himself to be crucified for sinners, as he had said he would: "I came to give my life a ransom for many."

Jesus went further, saying that he forgives more than sin's penalty, that his forgiveness embodies a total solution: freedom also from sin's guilt and sin's grip. "If the Son shall make you free (from sin), you shall be free indeed."

For people who in true repentance receive his forgiveness, Jesus claimed an ultimate benefit. With the estrangement (sin) between the believer and God removed, Jesus says he ushers him or her into a personal "relationship with God" and gives a desire and a power to live a godly life.

CHAPTER ELEVEN

Salvation by Grace

*E*very religion has at least two characteristics in common. Each purports that the moral/spiritual status of mankind falls short of being acceptable to its diety, leader or its ideal. Also each religion has devised a system whereby its followers can hopefully achieve progress toward such acceptability, or at least achieve some higher state of mind or moral perfection.

Typically the system for gaining acceptance from its leader or deity depends upon human self-effort for its success.

Jesus seems to have authored a radically different approach for becoming acceptable to God. His approach is based upon...

> Something *he* did, not upon something a human does;
>
> Something given to humans, not something earned by humans; and
>
> Something to be received, not something to be achieved.

Thus, followers of Jesus often quote, "Thanks be to God for His unspeakable gift," namely, the gift of Jesus.

Just what is Jesus' provision for making a human acceptable to the one who Jesus called the "one true God," God as described in the Old and New Testament scriptures?

In a word, Jesus died for the sins of humans. Because the universal core problem that renders humans unacceptable to God is sin, and because the penalty for sin is death, a human is powerless to pay sin's penalty, and yet live. It follows that if a person were to gain release from his sin and its penalty, it must be done for him. This Jesus claimed to do when he died for the sin of humans (Explanation in chapter 10). Being without sin, he was not under sin's penalty, hence could die for another. If Jesus was divine, his life did not have human limitations; hence his death could satisfy the sin problem for a limitless number of people.

The deliverance Jesus offers is called "salvation": salvation *from* sin, salvation *to* an inseparable union with God—now and forever. Because Jesus' loving gift was voluntary and for people who did not deserve this love, it was an act of "grace." Taken together, it is "salvation by grace."

The apostle Paul summarized, "By grace you are saved through faith…it is the gift of God."

This approach to God, offered by Jesus, has no parallel.

CHAPTER TWELVE

Supernatural Events Surrounding Death

Unprecedented events accompanied the death of Jesus. Of these, some were acts of nature, some were opponents' confessions, some were fulfilment of ages-old prophecies.

A. *Supernatural Acts of Nature.*

During the final three hours of Jesus' life on a cross, darkness covered the whole land. This was from noon to three o'clock. When Jesus called out with a loud voice, "It is finished," he died, and a violent rock-splitting earthquake thrust open the graves of some of the righteous deceased and ripped in two the veil in the temple. This several-inches-thick, heavily woven tapestry which had prevented access to the holy of holies (the place of God's presence) would be impossible for men to tear.

The brevity of the crucifixion event (when measured against the painfully lengthy death of a typical crucifixion), and the control over life that Jesus displayed by his early demise astonished onlookers. Typically, death by crucifixion took three to five days. A soldier thrust a sword into Jesus' side and, upon seeing water and blood flow out, pronounced Jesus dead after having been on the cross nine hours. Thereupon the Roman centurion, commander of the execution squad, and those that were with him, exclaimed, "Surely this was the Son of God."

B. Supernatural Confessions.

Another distinctive of the death events is that many of the people one would have expected to be among the first to build a case against Jesus instead proclaimed his innocence:

The traitor who was bribed to lead jealous religious leaders to Jesus repented and cried, "I have sinned in that I have betrayed innocent blood," and then committed suicide.

A ruler who was a member of the group that pressured Pilate to secure Jesus' sepulchre to prevent an escape, had privately told Jesus, "We know you are a teacher come from God."

The Roman governor, Pontius Pilate, who allowed Jesus to be crucified told the screaming crowd, "I have examined Jesus before you and find no fault in him"; "I am innocent of the blood of this just person."

Pilate's wife said to her husband, "Have nothing to do with that just man."

One of the thieves crucified alongside Jesus called out, "This man has done nothing wrong."

C. Supernatural Fulfilment.

Perhaps the two most curious elements about the events surrounding Jesus' death are that so many were the fulfilment of detailed prophecies written, recorded and preserved up to one thousand years, and that these events were performed by antagonists, the people who would never knowingly have validated Jesus' identity. Ancient Old Testament literature prophesied:

"Betrayed for thirty pieces of silver";

"Denied";

"Mocked";

"Laughed at";

"Spat upon";

"Accused falsely";

"Given gall for meat and vinegar for drink";

"Pierced in his hands and feet";

"Smitten on his back";

"No bone would be broken";

"Numbered with transgressors";

"His garments would be divided among people, but for his cloak they would cast lots"; and

"His grave would be with the wicked and the rich."

Observing these phenomena one asks, "Is it possible for a human to foretell accurately graphic details about the death of another human—a human who has not been born?"

How can one know these supernatural events really took place? Presumably the same way one knows that before Jesus' time on earth Alexander the Great led armies to conquer most of the civilized world and Plato published his philosophic discourses. The accounts of Jesus' life and death were written by competent historians: Matthew, Mark, the physician Luke and John, eyewitnesses known for careful attention to detail and for unembellished reporting. Across the centuries their writings have been acknowledged as reliable, even excellent records of the first century.

Individually, each of the death events above is a remarkable fulfilment of prophecy. Collectively, might they comprise compelling evidence that the one crucified was "History's Incomparable Man"?

CHAPTER THIRTEEN

The Resurrection

*A*part from Jesus, history knows nothing of a human being who predicted he would arise from the dead three days after dying—and then actually resurrect, physically, bodily.

Following crucifixion, Jesus was pronounced "dead" by professional executioners, wound tightly in linen cloths, immersed in embalming oil that hardened the linen in one hour, and placed in a tomb.

The record states that religious leaders, remembering Jesus' prior claim that he would arise from the dead and fearing the consequences to their own religion, persuaded Pilate, the Roman governor, to secure Jesus' sepulchre. He set a great stone (likely three thousand pounds) against the tomb entrance, sealed the cracks with wax and ordered soldiers (probably sixteen in number) to guard the sepulchre around the clock. Three days later the tomb was empty.

Nobody has offered a credible explanation for the empty tomb, apart from the one given by Jesus approximately one week before his death: namely, "The Son of Man shall be betrayed to the chief priest and to the scribes, and they shall condemn him to death, and shall deliver him to the Gentiles to mock, and to scourge, and to *crucify him*, and the *third day he shall rise again*."

Did Jesus' resurrection really happen? It appears…

> The guards believed it. They ran back and told the chief priests what had happened.
>
> The Sanhedrin (religious leaders) believed it. Fearing defection of their followers, they bribed the soldiers and Pilate to say the soldiers

had fallen asleep (the penalty for which was death) and Jesus' disciples had stolen the body.

Eyewitnesses believed it. Jesus showed himself to several on the third day following his death, and on at least ten other occasions across the following forty days to others in different locales. On one occasion, five hundred people saw the resurrected Jesus. He conversed, he ate, he let people touch him to prove he was not a ghost. As a result, many eyewitnesses left their vocations permanently and traveled widely throughout Europe and Asia telling of Jesus' resurrection. Disbelievers accused them of "turning the world upside down." The price of this outspoken witness was usually opposition and eventual martyrdom.

Contemporaries in Jerusalem believed it. The apostle Paul challenged King Agrippa, "The king knows of these things...none of these things are hidden from you, for this thing (resurrection) was not done in a corner."

Scholars believe it. Historian John A. Broadus (Seminary president and professor of New

Testament Interpretation) has been quoted, "The resurrection of Jesus is the best attested fact in early annals. By all the laws of historical evidence, it is true. If we do not know this, we know nothing in ancient history."

This phenomenon which some call "the hinge of history" was anticipated by King David approximately one thousand years before the event, when claiming to be writing under the direction of God, he foretold the resurrection of God's Holy One.

Why did the resurrection happen? Jesus gave four reasons, before the event:

To fulfil scripture that had foretold the event;

To prove he had power to vanquish humanity's worst enemy, sin/death;

To prove he is who he said he is; and

To prove his word is true, worthy of trust.

Two years before Jesus' death, after seeing some of his miracles, sceptics asked Jesus to give them a "sign" that they might be sure who he really was. Jesus replied, "Only one sign will be given you:

destroy this temple [i.e., my body] and in three days I will raise it up." From this, one can see that Jesus predicated his entire life and ministry on the reality of his eventual resurrection.

Has there been any teacher before or since who has invited others to assess his life and teaching "a fraud" unless he could perform a supernatural feat never-before accomplished, specifically rising bodily from the dead?

Another consequence that flows from the resurrection is that whereas all other of history's famous leaders are dead, Jesus must be alive—from the dead.

CHAPTER FOURTEEN

Kingdom of Love

"Alexander, Caesar, Charlemagne and I founded empires upon force. Jesus founded his empire on love." So Emperor Napoleon reportedly said.

Others have built their kingdoms on heredity or military might, ideas or religious fear. Unique among kingdom-builders, Jesus' three years of ministry were marked by acts of love: love of God, love of man and woman, love of the lofty and the lonely, those well and those suffering, those appreciative and those hostile. Jesus pictured his coming to earth to be a great act of love, his death to be the supreme act of love, "Greater love has no man than this, that he give his life for his friend." Jesus apparently had nothing to gain, only something to give. He said he gave his life that others might live—live eternally with a loving God.

Jesus' kingdom is held together by love.

No human force compels one to enter Jesus' kingdom. No coercion requires one to stay in his kingdom.

People are drawn to Jesus by his love. People continue their allegiance out of love for him, though they are humanly free to leave his kingdom at any time.

Jesus' kingdom expresses itself in love.

Jesus said, "Hereby will men know you are my disciples, that you have love one for another."

History shows that members of his kingdom have generated more hospitals, orphanages, schools, hospices, human relief organizations and missionaries than have all other groups of earth's people together.

One illustration of this compassion is the internationally appreciated Red Cross organization. Reportedly, its founders selected the cross for their symbol, emblematic of Christ's sacrifice of his life for others, and the color red to represent his blood shed to atone for sin, life's chief act of mercy.

Because of such observations, some people say Jesus' life is preeminently summed up by the well-known Bible verse: "God so LOVED the world that he gave his only begotten son, that whosoever believes in him shall not perish, but have everlasting life."

CHAPTER FIFTEEN

Second Coming

*A*nother issue which seems to set Jesus apart from every sane historical figure is the promise of a future action never before achieved, namely, "I will come again" (to earth). This promise was coupled with considerable detail.

When he departed earth in an unprecedented manner—bodily ascending from the midst of several people into the clouds—two angels appeared declaring, "This same Jesus, which is taken up into heaven, shall so come in like manner [bodily] as you have seen him go into heaven."

Two millennia have passed since this promise. Jesus has not returned to earth bodily, in like manner. Whether he will is yet to be seen.

On hearing this promise people, then and now, ask: "When?" "How?" "Why?" Jesus' reply to these three questions was recorded.

When will Jesus return? Unexpectedly, Jesus said. "Of that day and that hour no man knows, but my father only, not even the angels which are in heaven. Take heed, be ready, for the Son of man comes suddenly, at an hour you think not."

How will Jesus return? "There shall be false Christs and false prophets. People will say, 'He is here,' 'He is there.' Do not be deceived. Believe them not." He said everybody, everywhere would recognize his coming because it would be attended by cataclysmic events. "The sun shall be darkened, the moon shall not give her light, the stars of heaven shall fall, the powers that are in heaven shall be shaken. And then all peoples of the earth shall see the Son of Man coming in the clouds with the angels in great power and glory." "As the lightning comes out of the east and shines even unto the west, so shall also the coming of the Son of Man be in his day." Jesus spoke these claims simply, clearly, confidently and without embellishment.

Why will Jesus return? In his words:

> To Love (his own). "I will come again and receive you unto myself, that where I am there you may be also."

> To Reward. "I come quickly. My reward is with me, to give every man according as his work shall be."

> To Separate. "He shall sit upon the throne of his glory. All peoples shall be gathered before him, and he shall separate them one from another, the righteous from the unrighteous."

> To Ordain. "To the righteous, he will say, 'Inherit life eternal in the kingdom of my

Father.' To the unrighteous, he will say, 'Go away to everlasting punishment.'"

To Renew. "He will sit upon the throne and say, 'I make all things new...a new heaven and a new earth.'"

To Reign. "The kingdoms of this world will become the kingdom of our Lord. He shall reign for ever and ever."

To Dwell. "I will dwell with them (believers), and be their God."

One may ask, "Has any man on earth—before or since—spoken so loftily, so comprehensively, so authoritatively about the future?" It is too early to test the historical accuracy of these statements. Yet, it is noteworthy that all of Jesus' prophetic utterances which were to have occurred as of this time have come to pass; none has failed.

Conclusion

The conclusion to this handbook will necessarily be "written by the reader." When one hears of an earthly life lived supernaturally—in terms of birth, omniscience, miracles, resurrection and prophetic accuracy—one is inescapably faced with two questions, and two decisions.

First, "Was there a life lived on this planet two thousand years ago that was inherently unique to all others?" Once informed by the historical facts about Jesus, the answer to this question comes quite readily. The credentials of none other can compare. His credentials cannot be duplicated. This must be "History's Incomparable Man!"

The second and greater question begging a conclusion is, "Who really was (is) this Incomparable Man?" Might he be the Lord? The way in which one answers this question will inevitably determine one's life-course, one's destiny.

What conclusions were drawn by those who observed Jesus' life most closely?

> Peter: "We believe and are sure you are the Christ, the Son of the living God."
> Nicodemus: (Ruler of Jews, member of religious Pharisees that pressured Governor Pilate for Jesus' crucifixion) "We know you are come from God; no one can do these miracles you do except God be with him."
> Matthew: "Jesus the Christ, the son of David, the son of Abraham."
> Martha: "Lord, I believe you are the Christ, the Son of God, which should come into the world."

Thomas: "My Lord and my God," upon touching the resurrected Jesus.
John: "Who is a liar, but he who denies that Jesus is the Christ?"
Paul: "The resurrection declares Jesus to be the Son of God with power."

To people who heard and saw him, Jesus asked, "Who do *you* say I am?"

Doubtless Jesus would ask the same '*pivotal question of life*' to all who through this book learn of his distinctives, **"Who do YOU say I am?"**

About the Author

William C. Savage is a self-employed businessman with a Bachelor of Science degree from Stanford University (Economics & Business Law). He has been graced with fifty years of marriage to Betty. They have two children and six grandchildren.

Having an inquisitive, analytical mind, Mr. Savage has given a lifetime to investigating carefully life's most penetrating questions: "What is humankind's purpose and destiny?", "Amidst the world's plethora of voices, is there any one person who speaks with unique authority, who gives ultimate answers instead of opinions?" This pursuit included two years of advanced studies at Fuller Theological Seminary. Across the years Mr. Savage has shared his studies with thousands of collegians, high-schoolers and adults of all ages.

Jesus: History's Incomparable Man?
Order Form

Postal Orders: The Cornerstone Trust
P.O. Box 1050
Carefree, AZ 85377

With orders, please include the following information for recipients:

Name: _____

Address: _____

City: _____ State: _____

Zip: _____

Telephone: (_____) _____

Book Price: $7.99 (The price is subject to change without notice.)

Shipping: $3.00 for the first book and $1.00 for each additional book to cover shipping and handling within US, Canada, and Mexico. International orders add $6.00 for the first book and $2.00 for each additional book

Or order from:
ACW Press
5501 N. 7th. Ave. #502
Phoenix, AZ 85013

(800) 931-BOOK

or contact your local bookstore